COMPOSER SHOWCASE
HAL LEONARD STUDENT PIANO LIBRARY

EARLY INTERMEDIATE/INTERMEDIATE LEVEL

Christmas Impressions

NINE TRADITIONAL CAROLS FOR PIANO SOLO

ARRANGED BY JENNIFER LINN

*I dedicate this book to Mark Linn, my husband of 25 years,
in a loving tribute to our marriage and the power of God's love.*

CONTENTS

ISBN-13: 978-1-4234-3168-8

HAL•LEONARD®
CORPORATION
7777 W. BLUEMOUND RD. P.O. BOX 13819 MILWAUKEE, WI 53213

In Australia Contact:
Hal Leonard Australia Pty. Ltd.
4 Lentara Court
Cheltenham, Victoria, 3192 Australia
Email: ausadmin@halleonard.com

Visit Hal Leonard Online at
www.halleonard.com

Carol Of The Bells

Ukrainian Christmas Carol
Arranged by Jennifer Linn

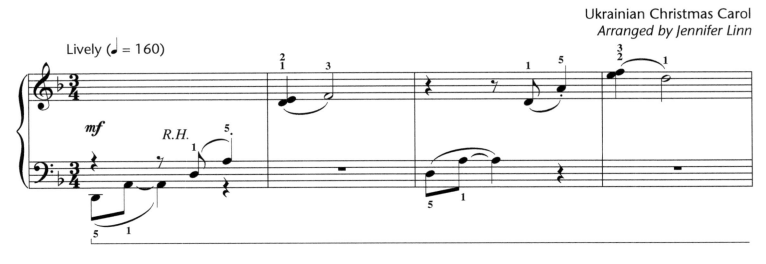

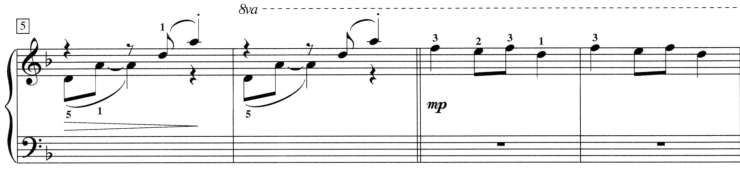

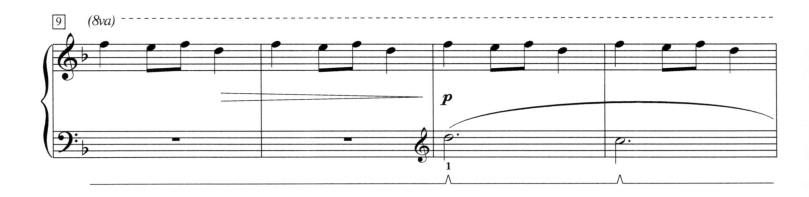

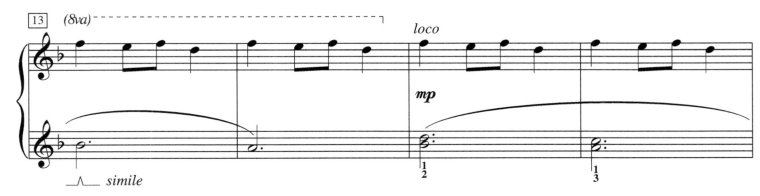

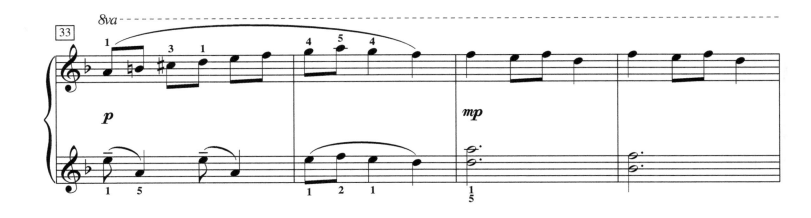

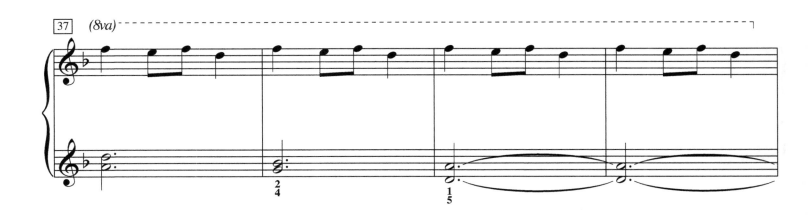

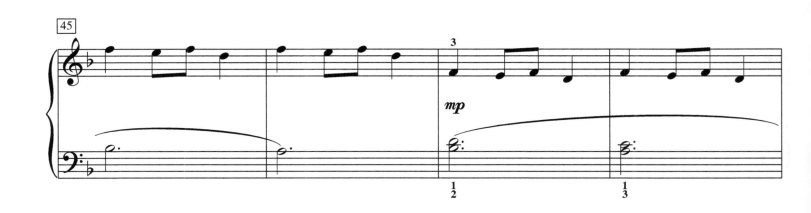

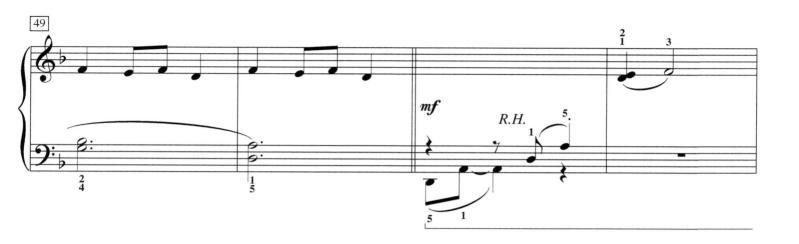

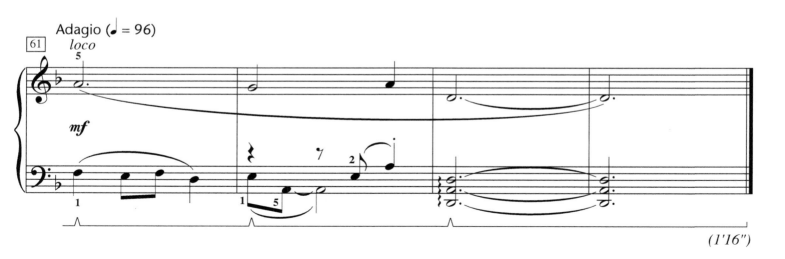

Coventry Carol

Words by Robert Croo
Traditional English Melody
Arranged by Jennifer Linn

He Is Born, The Holy Child

(Il est né, le Divin Enfant)

Traditional French Carol
Arranged by Jennifer Linn

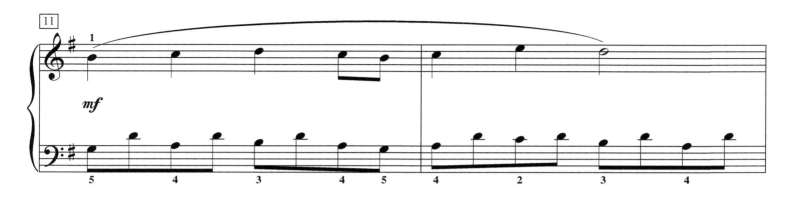

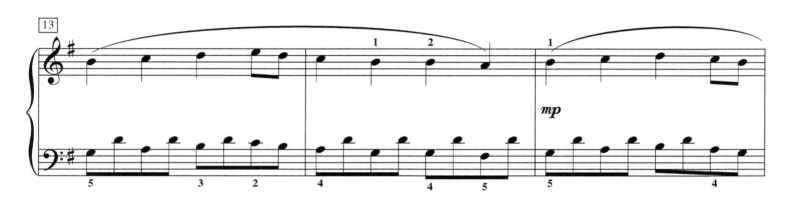

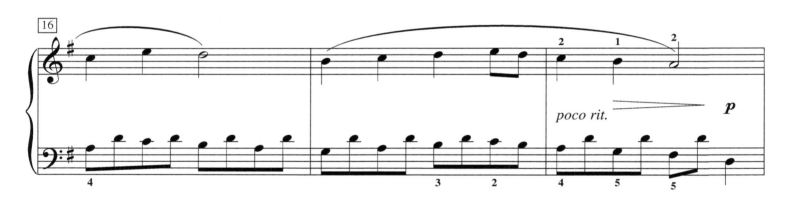

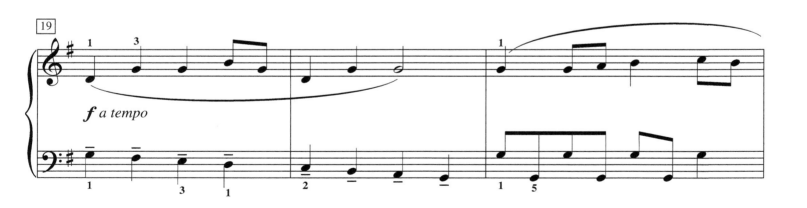

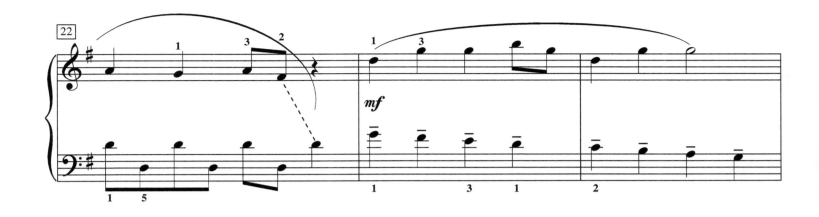

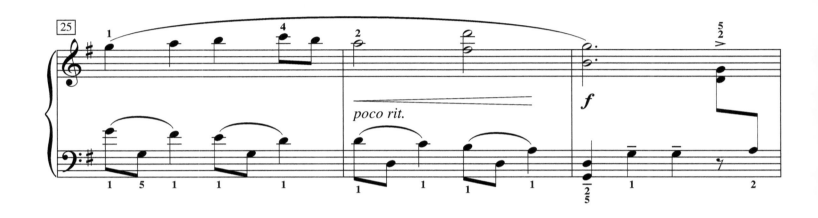

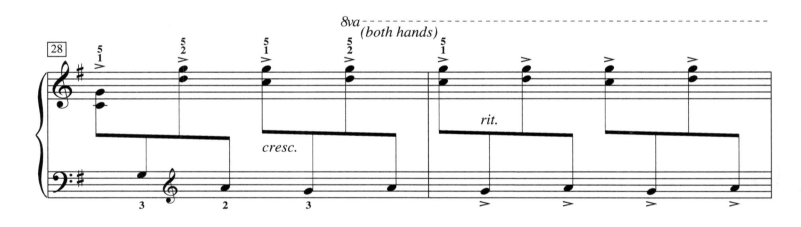

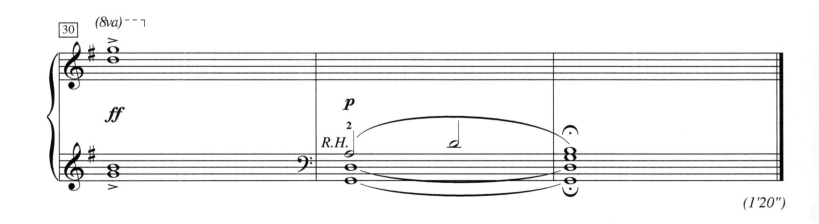

(1'20")

Jumpin' Jingle Bells

Words and Music by J. Pierpont
Arranged by Jennifer Linn

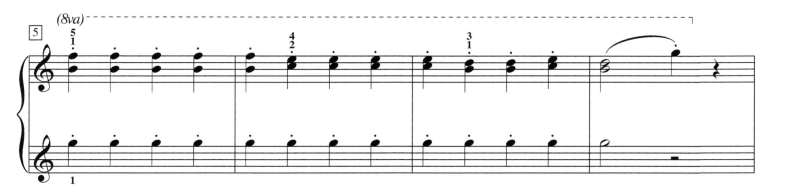

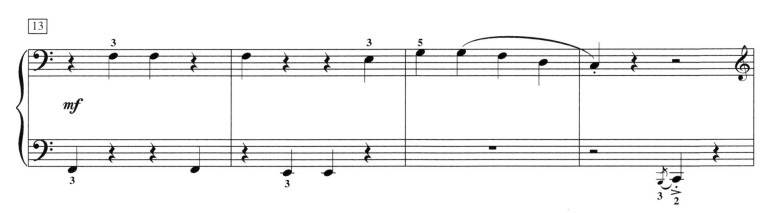

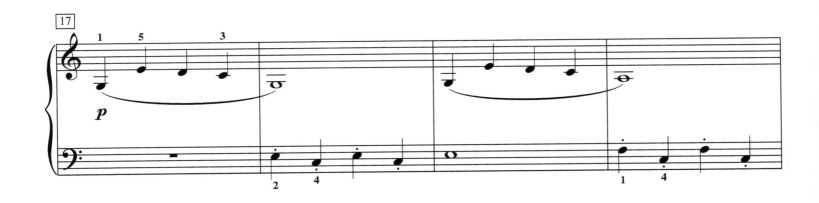

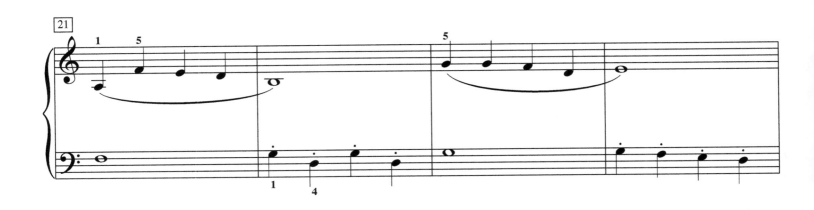

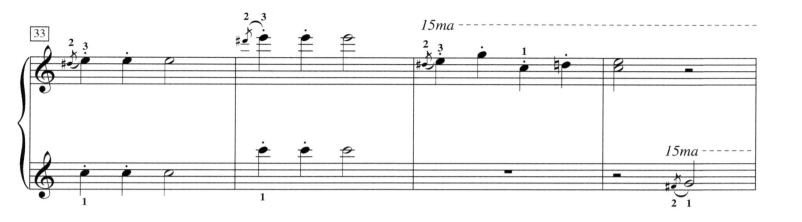

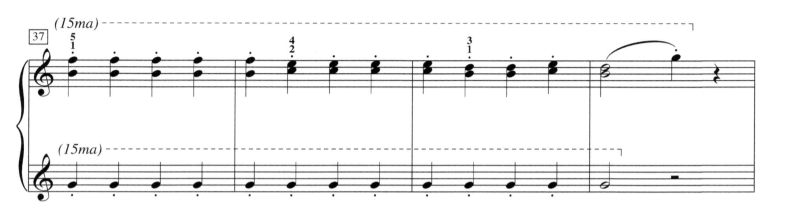

(1'08")

O Come, All Ye Faithful

Music by John Francis Wade
Arranged by Jennifer Linn

Moderato (♩ = 138)

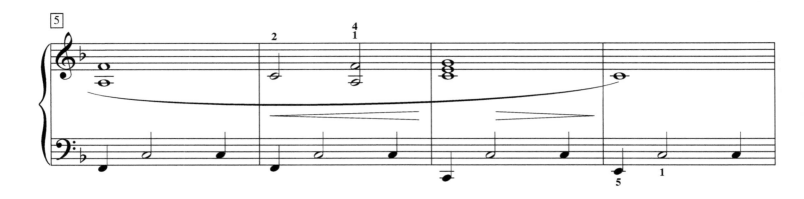

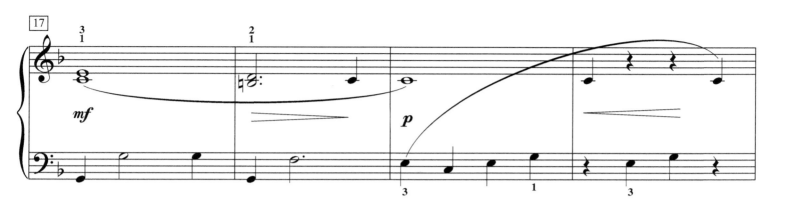

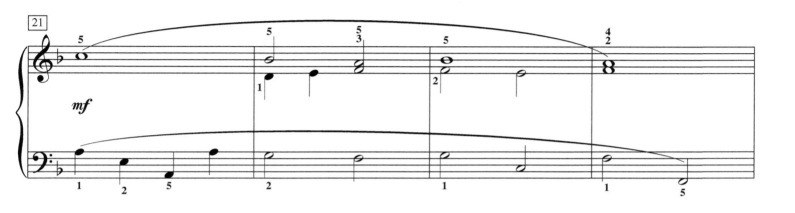

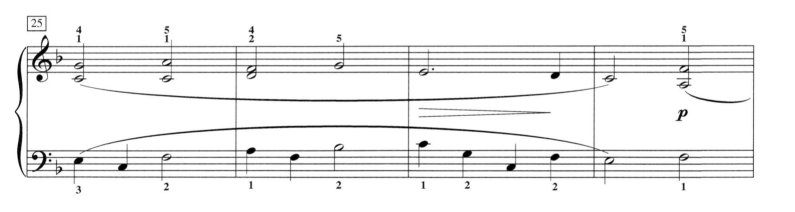

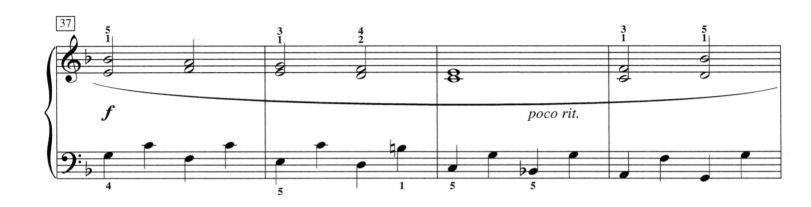

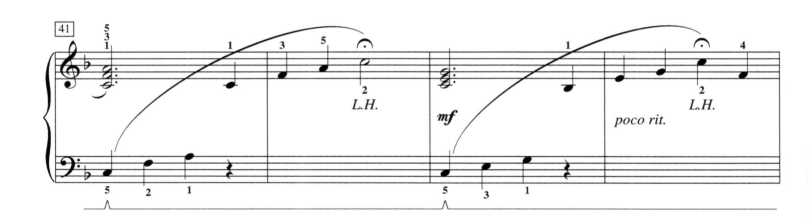

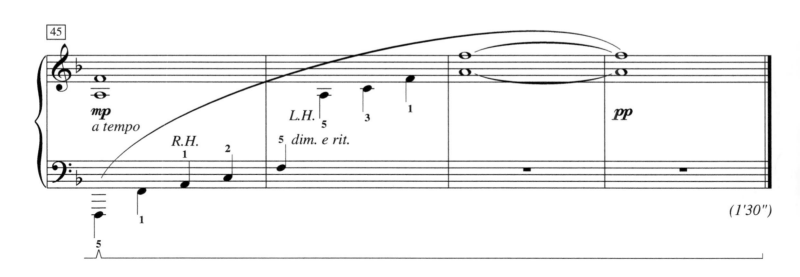

(1'30")

Pat-a-Pan
(Willie, Take Your Little Drum)

Words and Music by
Bernard de la Monnoye
Arranged by Jennifer Linn

Steady and calm (♩ = 144)

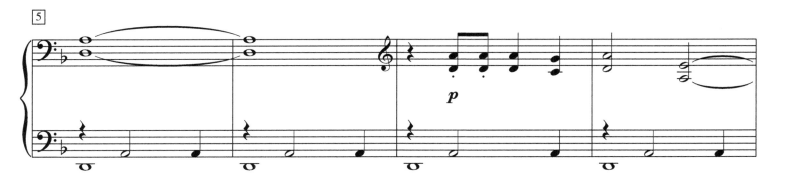

With pedal

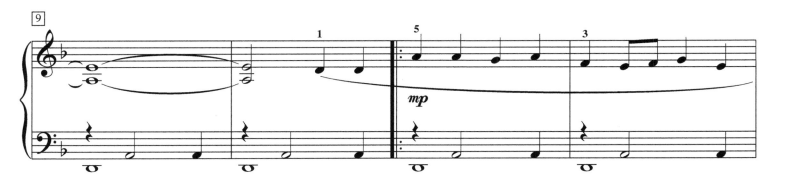

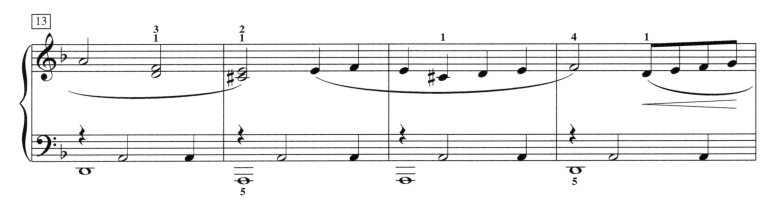

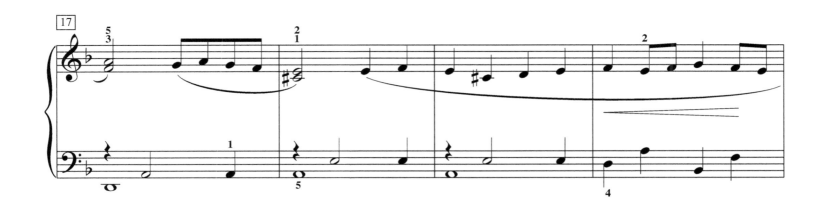

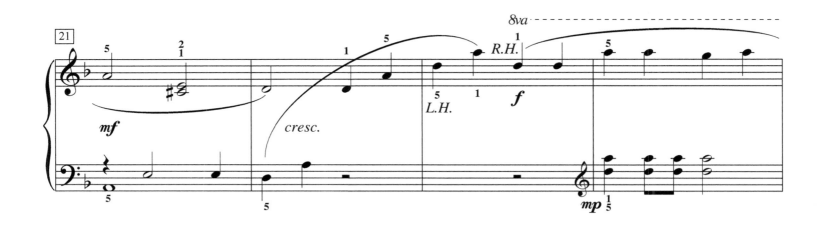

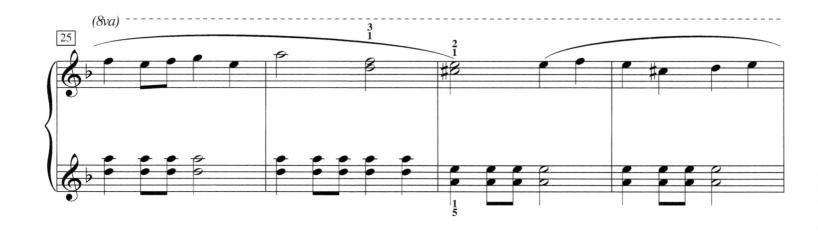

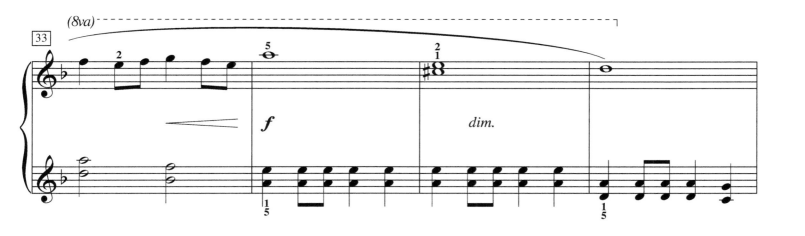

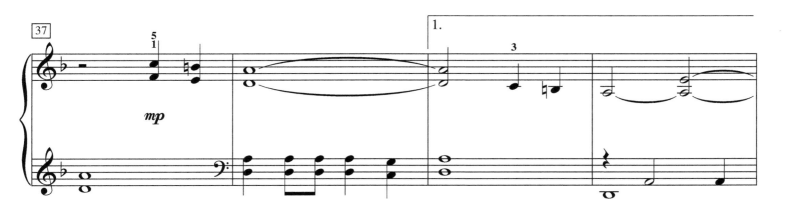

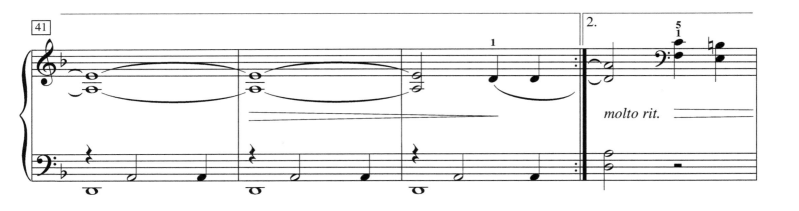

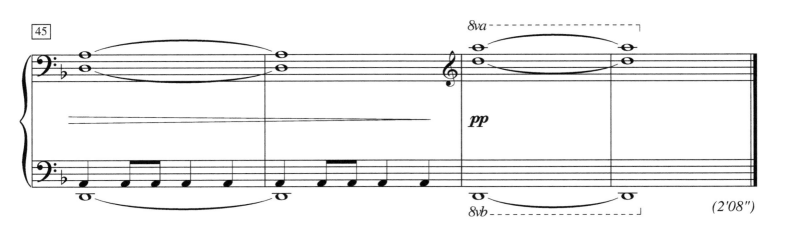

(2'08")

O Holy Night

French Words by Placide Cappeau
English Words by John S. Dwight
Music by Adolphe Adam
Arranged by Jennifer Linn

Andante con moto (♪. = 54)

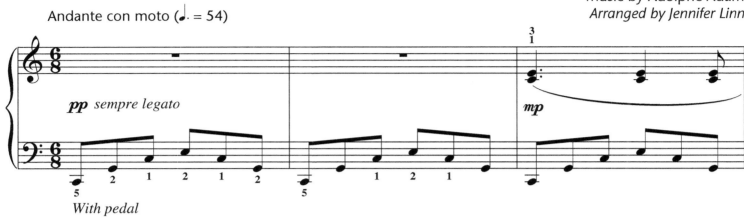

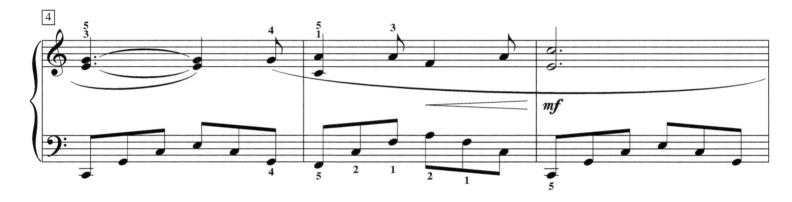

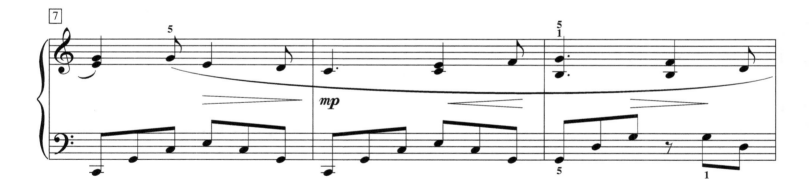

23

Silent Night

Words by Joseph Mohr
Translated by John F. Young
Music by Franz X. Gruber
Arranged by Jennifer Linn

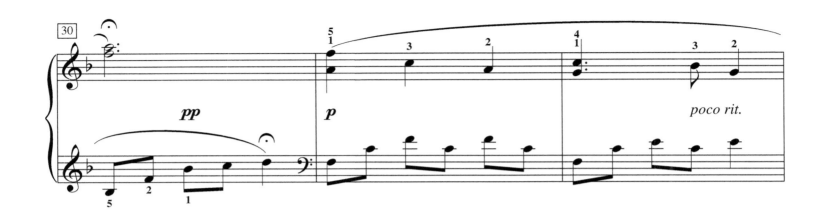

(3'05")

What Child Is This?

Words by William C. Dix
16th Century English Melody
Arranged by Jennifer Linn

Dolce, cantabile (♩ = 108)

(2'08")

Carol Of The Bells *(Page 2)*

Hark to the bells, hark to the bells,
Telling us all Jesus is King!
Strongly they chime, sound with a rhyme,
Christmas is here, welcome the King.

Hark to the bells, hark to the bells,
This is the day, day of the King!
Peal out the news o'er hill and dale,
And 'round the town telling the tale.

Hark to the bells, hark to the bells,
Telling us all Jesus is King!
Come, one and all happily sing
Songs of good will, O let them sing!

Ring, silv'ry bells, sing, joyous bells!
Strongly they chime, sound with a rhyme,
Christmas is here, welcome the King!

Hark to the bells, hark to the bells,
Telling us all Jesus is King! Ring! Ring! bells.

Coventry Carol *(Page 6)*

Lullay, thou little tiny Child,
By by, lully, lullay.
Lullay, thou little tiny Child,
By by, lully, lullay.

O sisters too, how may we do,
For to preserve this day.
This poor youngling for whom we sing.
By by, lully, lullay.

He Is Born, The Holy Child (Il est né, Divin Enfant)
(Page 8)

He is born, the Holy Child,
Play the oboe and bagpipes merrily!
He is born, the Holy Child,
Sing we all of the Savior mild.

Through long ages of the past,
Prophets have betold His coming;
Through long ages of the past,
Now the time has come at last!

Refrain
Jesus, Lord of all the world,
Coming as a Child among us;
Jesus, Lord of all the world,
Grant to us Thy heav'nly peace.

O how lovely, O how pure,
Is this perfect Child of heaven;
O how lovely, O how pure,
Gracious gift of God to man!

Jumpin' Jingle Bells *(Page 11)*

Dashing through the snow in a one-horse
   open sleigh,
O'er the fields we go, laughing all the way.
Bells on bobtail ring, making spirits bright,
What fun it is to ride and sing a sleighing
   song tonight! Oh!

Refrain
Jingle bells, jingle bells, jingle all the way.
Oh what fun it is to ride in a one-horse
   open sleigh!
Jingle bells, jingle bells, jingle all the way.
Oh what fun it is to ride in a one-horse
   open sleigh!

O Come, All Ye Faithful
(Page 14)

O come, all ye faithful, joyful and
   triumphant,
O come ye, O come ye to Bethlehem.
Come and behold Him, born the King
   of angels.

Refrain
O come let us adore Him, O come let us
   adore Him,
O come let us adore Him, Christ the Lord.

Sing choirs of angels, sing in exultation,
Sing, all ye citizens of heaven above.
Glory to God in the highest.

Yea, Lord, we greet Thee, born this happy
   morning,
Jesus, to Thee be all glory giv'n.
Word of the Father, now in flesh appearing.

Pat-a-Pan *(Page 17)*

Willie, take your little drum,
Robin, bring your whistle, come.
When we hear the fife and drum,
Tu-re-lu-re-lu, pat-a-pat-a-pan.
When we hear the fife and drum,
Christmas should be light and fun.

Thus the men of olden days
Gave the King of kings their praise.
When they hear the fife and drum,
Tu-re-lu-re-lu, pat-a-pat-a-pan.
With the drums they sing and play,
Full of joy on Christmas day.

God and man are now become
Closely joined as fife and drum.
When we play the fife and drum,
Tu-re-lu-re-lu, pat-a-pat-a-pan.
When on fife and drum we play,
Dance and make the holiday.

O Holy Night *(Page 20)*

O holy night, the stars are brightly shining,
It is the night of the dear Savior's birth.
Long lay the world in sin and error pining,
Till He appeared and the soul felt its worth.
A thrill of hope, the weary world rejoices,
For yonder breaks a new and glorious morn;
Fall on your knees! O, hear the angel voices!
O night divine, O night when Christ was born!
O night, O holy night, O night divine!

Truly He taught us to love one another,
His law is love, and His gospel is peace.
Chains shall He break, for the slave is our
   brother,
And in His name all oppression shall cease.
Sweet hymns of joy in grateful chorus
   raise we,
Let all within us praise His holy name;
Christ is the Lord, O praise His name
   forever!
His pow'r and glory ever more proclaim!
His pow'r and glory ever more proclaim!

Silent Night *(Page 24)*

Silent night, holy night!
All is calm, all is bright.
Round yon Virgin Mother and Child.
Holy Infant so tender and mild,
Sleep in heavenly peace,
Sleep in heavenly peace.

Silent night, holy night!
Shepherds quake at the sight.
Glories stream from heaven afar,
Heavenly hosts sing Alleluia,
Christ the Savior is born!
Christ the Savior is born.

Silent night, holy night!
Son of God, love's pure light.
Radiant beams from Thy holy face
With the dawn of redeeming grace,
Jesus, Lord, at Thy birth.
Jesus, Lord, at Thy birth.

What Child Is This? *(Page 27)*

What Child is this, who, laid to rest,
On Mary's lap is sleeping?
Whom angels greet with anthems sweet,
While shepherds watch are keeping?

Refrain
This, this is Christ the King,
Whom shepherds guard and angels sing:
Haste, haste to bring Him laud,
The Babe, the Son of Mary.

Why lies He in such mean estate
Where ox and ass are feeding?
Good Christian, fear, for sinners here
The silent Word is pleading.

So bring Him incense, gold, and myrrh,
Come peasant, king to own Him;
The King of kings salvation brings,
Let loving hearts enthrone Him.

This series showcases great original piano music from our **Hal Leonard Student Piano Library** family of composers. Carefully graded for easy selection.

BILL BOYD

JAZZ BITS (AND PIECES)
Early Intermediate Level
00290312 11 Solos........................$7.99

JAZZ DELIGHTS
Intermediate Level
00240435 11 Solos........................$8.99

JAZZ FEST
Intermediate Level
00240436 10 Solos........................$8.99

JAZZ PRELIMS
Early Elementary Level
00290032 12 Solos........................$7.99

JAZZ SKETCHES
Intermediate Level
00220001 8 Solos........................$8.99

JAZZ STARTERS
Elementary Level
00290425 10 Solos........................$8.99

JAZZ STARTERS II
Late Elementary Level
00290434 11 Solos........................$7.99

JAZZ STARTERS III
Late Elementary Level
00290465 12 Solos........................$8.99

THINK JAZZ!
Early Intermediate Level
00290417 Method Book............$12.99

TONY CARAMIA

JAZZ MOODS
Intermediate Level
00296728 8 Solos........................$6.95

SUITE DREAMS
Intermediate Level
00296775 4 Solos........................$6.99

SONDRA CLARK

DAKOTA DAYS
Intermediate Level
00296521 5 Solos........................$6.95

FLORIDA FANTASY SUITE
Intermediate Level
00296766 3 Duets........................$7.95

THREE ODD METERS
Intermediate Level
00296472 3 Duets........................$6.95

MATTHEW EDWARDS

CONCERTO FOR YOUNG PIANISTS
FOR 2 PIANOS, FOUR HANDS
Intermediate Level Book/CD
00296356 3 Movements $19.99

CONCERTO NO. 2 IN G MAJOR
FOR 2 PIANOS, 4 HANDS
Intermediate Level Book/CD
00296670 3 Movements............$17.99

PHILLIP KEVEREN

MOUSE ON A MIRROR
Late Elementary Level
00296361 5 Solos........................$8.99

MUSICAL MOODS
Elementary/Late Elementary Level
00296714 7 Solos........................$6.99

SHIFTY-EYED BLUES
Late Elementary Level
00296374 5 Solos........................$7.99

CAROL KLOSE

THE BEST OF CAROL KLOSE
Early to Late Intermediate Level
00146151 15 Solos....................$12.99

CORAL REEF SUITE
Late Elementary Level
00296354 7 Solos........................$7.50

DESERT SUITE
Intermediate Level
00296667 6 Solos........................$7.99

FANCIFUL WALTZES
Early Intermediate Level
00296473 5 Solos........................$7.95

GARDEN TREASURES
Late Intermediate Level
00296787 5 Solos........................$8.50

ROMANTIC EXPRESSIONS
Intermediate to Late Intermediate Level
00296923 5 Solos........................$8.99

WATERCOLOR MINIATURES
Early Intermediate Level
00296848 7 Solos........................$7.99

JENNIFER LINN

AMERICAN IMPRESSIONS
Intermediate Level
00296471 6 Solos........................$8.99

ANIMALS HAVE FEELINGS TOO
Early Elementary/Elementary Level
00147789 8 Solos........................$8.99

AU CHOCOLAT
Late Elementary/Early Intermediate Level
00298110 7 Solos........................$8.99

CHRISTMAS IMPRESSIONS
Intermediate Level
00296706 8 Solos........................$8.99

JUST PINK
Elementary Level
00296722 9 Solos........................$8.99

LES PETITES IMAGES
Late Elementary Level
00296664 7 Solos........................$8.99

LES PETITES IMPRESSIONS
Intermediate Level
00296355 6 Solos........................$8.99

REFLECTIONS
Late Intermediate Level
00296843 5 Solos........................$8.99

TALES OF MYSTERY
Intermediate Level
00296769 6 Solos........................$8.99

LYNDA LYBECK-ROBINSON

ALASKA SKETCHES
Early Intermediate Level
00119637 8 Solos........................$8.99

AN AWESOME ADVENTURE
Late Elementary Level
00137563 8 Solos........................$7.99

FOR THE BIRDS
Early Intermediate/Intermediate Level
00237078 9 Solos........................$8.99

WHISPERING WOODS
Late Elementary Level
00275905 9 Solos........................$8.99

MONA REJINO

CIRCUS SUITE
Late Elementary Level
00296665 5 Solos........................$8.99

COLOR WHEEL
Early Intermediate Level
00201951 6 Solos........................$9.99

IMPRESIONES DE ESPAÑA
Intermediate Level
00337520 6 Solos........................$8.99

IMPRESSIONS OF NEW YORK
Intermediate Level
00364212........................$8.99

JUST FOR KIDS
Elementary Level
00296840 8 Solos........................$7.99

MERRY CHRISTMAS MEDLEYS
Intermediate Level
00296799 5 Solos........................$8.99

MINIATURES IN STYLE
Intermediate Level
00148088 6 Solos........................$8.99

PORTRAITS IN STYLE
Early Intermediate Level
00296507 6 Solos........................$8.99

EUGÉNIE ROCHEROLLE

CELEBRATION SUITE
Intermediate Level
00152724 3 Duets........................$8.99

ENCANTOS ESPAÑOLES (SPANISH DELIGHTS)
Intermediate Level
00125451 6 Solos........................$8.99

JAMBALAYA
Intermediate Level
00296654 2 Pianos, 8 Hands.....$12.99
00296725 2 Pianos, 4 Hands.......$7.95

JEROME KERN CLASSICS
Intermediate Level
00296577 10 Solos....................$12.99

LITTLE BLUES CONCERTO
Early Intermediate Level
00142801 2 Pianos, 4 Hands......$12.99

TOUR FOR TWO
Late Elementary Level
00296832 6 Duets........................$9.99

TREASURES
Late Elementary/Early Intermediate Level
00296924 7 Solos........................$8.99

JEREMY SISKIND

BIG APPLE JAZZ
Intermediate Level
00278209 8 Solos........................$8.99

MYTHS AND MONSTERS
Late Elementary/Early Intermediate Level
00148148 9 Solos........................$8.99

CHRISTOS TSITSAROS

DANCES FROM AROUND THE WORLD
Early Intermediate Level
00296688 7 Solos........................$8.99

FIVE SUMMER PIECES
Late Intermediate/Advanced Level
00361235 5 Solos........................$12.99

LYRIC BALLADS
Intermediate/Late Intermediate Level
00102404 6 Solos........................$8.99

POETIC MOMENTS
Intermediate Level
00296403 8 Solos........................$8.99

SEA DIARY
Early Intermediate Level
00253486 9 Solos........................$8.99

SONATINA HUMORESQUE
Late Intermediate Level
00296772 3 Movements.............$6.99

SONGS WITHOUT WORDS
Intermediate Level
00296506 9 Solos........................$9.99

THREE PRELUDES
Early Advanced Level
00130747 3 Solos........................$8.99

THROUGHOUT THE YEAR
Late Elementary Level
00296723 12 Duets....................$6.95

ADDITIONAL COLLECTIONS

AT THE LAKE
by Elvina Pearce
Elementary/Late Elementary Level
00131642 10 Solos and Duets.....$7.99

CHRISTMAS FOR TWO
by Dan Fox
Early Intermediate Level
00290069 13 Duets....................$8.99

CHRISTMAS JAZZ
by Mike Springer
Intermediate Level
00296525 6 Solos........................$8.99

COUNTY RAGTIME FESTIVAL
by Fred Kern
Intermediate Level
00296882 7 Solos........................$7.99

LITTLE JAZZERS
by Jennifer Watts
Elementary/Late Elementary Level
00154573 9 Solos........................$8.99

PLAY THE BLUES!
by Luann Carman
Early Intermediate Level
00296357 10 Solos........................$9.99

ROLLER COASTERS & RIDES
by Jennifer & Mike Watts
Intermediate Level
00131144 8 Duets........................$8.99